Auras

poems by

Douglas Nordfors

Plain View Press
P. O. 42255
Austin, TX 78704

plainviewpress.net
sb@plainviewpress.net
1-512-441-2452

Copyright Douglas Nordfors 2008. All rights reserved.
ISBN: 978-0-911051-40-7
Library of Congress Number: 2008940975

Cover painting by Beverly Goodrum.

Acknowledgements

The following poems have appeared, sometimes in slightly different versions, in the following journals:

"Pony Ride" in *California Quarterly*; "Animal Behavior" in *Cream City Review*; "Shelter" in *The Hampden-Sydney Poetry Review*; "24 Hours," "A Dog's Life" and "The Slaughter Of Elephants" in *The Iowa Review*; "With Loneliness" in *Karamu*; "Lines" in *The Lucid Stone*; "Tess Of The D'Urbervilles" in *Quarterly West*; "In Pursuit Of A Theme" in *Reed Magazine*; and "Sioux Hunters: Photograph By Edward S. Curtis" in *The Seattle Review*.

Contents

Acknowledgements   2

Children's Story   5

    Pony Ride   7
    Central Park Children's Zoo   8
    Brooklyn Botanic Garden   9
    Children's Story   10
    The Land of the Living   14
    The Journals of Lewis and Clark   17
    What Do You Say?   18
    An Inkling   19
    Child at Heart   20
    Lachrymose   22

The World   25

    The World   27
    The Slaughter of Elephants   28
    The Hole in the Ozone Layer   30
    Elegy for Dian Fossey   31
    Auras   33
    A Photograph of Mount Rainer   35
    Why Did the Turtle Cross the Road?   38
    True Love   39
    Extinct   41
    Nature Poem   42

In Pursuit of a Theme   43

    Animal Behavior   45
    Shelter   47
    Tess of the D'Urbervilles   48
    The Ocean   49
    In Pursuit of a Theme   50
    The Living   52

The One Church	53
God and Nature	54
First Visit to Walden Pond	55
Second Visit to Walden Pond	57

Green   59

Cycle	61
Green	62
Blight	63
24 Hours	64
Sioux Hunters: Photograph by Edward S. Curtis	65
My Mind's Eye	66
A Dog's Life	67
With Loneliness	68
Whale Watching	69
Sentimentality	71

Romantic   73

Tree Farm	75
Glen Nevis	76
Lines	78
Above Grasmere	79
Romantic	80
Nature Lover	81
My Pasture	82
The Woman at the Washington Zoo	83
Yes	84
Chant	85

About the Author	87

Children's Story

Pony Ride

You can ask your past to do anything, and so
it was yesterday that I rode that pony

that stallion for a quarter, and he would have
cared if I had never just sat on him,

did nothing, covered distance like grass,
gazed with joy at my warrior's hand on his mane.

○

You can ask your past to do anything, and so
I gripped the saddle with both hands,

relived every scar on my knees.
My eyes actually burned with fear.

I was the smallest sun

the earth could ever revolve around
without irreparably turning to ice.

○

I haven't forgotten the girl who led the pony,
who talked to him simply, as if to a child,

using words I pretended I didn't know.
All three of us made it all the way around the circle.

Now I think: The girl was talking to me
when she talked like that to the pony, so softly...the tenderness

the whole world dreams of, even
when one of us experiences it.

Central Park Children's Zoo

The space between the hand of a city
kid and the downy head of a young goat is
as far as I can see the secret of life.

I don't stop there. I wait for
the hand to touch. There. I keep waiting.
For the murder rate to scrape bottom.

For prisons to be torn down. For idealism
to hit a wall, burst into the clear. For
the moon's fire in my hands, the sun's fire

out of my hands to form a hollow.
I will be safe there. Gentleness
will take my life. There I will rest.

Brooklyn Botanic Garden

On the way here I saw three boys aiming empty
bottles at car windows and following through.

Like a born army, they marched down what could be
the smallest street in all of Brooklyn, their

mission to spread the terror of the world
they feel inside out under the sky's limit.

I have this idea:

If anyone was looking, I would place on the gravel path
a little dish of water

laced with my blood,
and sparrows would

do a dance around it,
terrified to drink.

I have this idea:

If anyone was looking, I would walk off the gravel path,
not even to pick, just to touch

the flowers, and the flowers,
who have no beliefs,

would cease to believe.

Children's Story

                                      Once
        upon a time
                way up in the sky Eagle
wondered if his wings could work without his heart into them

                          way up in the sky
              farther than the eye can tell
                    he let himself go
and wondered if the ground would touch him

                          this
           isn't his story
                  Stray Dog was trotting along
when he saw Eagle falling and falling out of the sky

                          Stray Dog couldn't
        swallow his own life
                he looked around him
the air was invisible and there was moss on the stones

                      embedded
        in the shallow river
                he thought of the man
who would leave him alone in the empty house for the longest time

                    then give him food
        and talk to him in a voice
                that moved in all directions
toward a happiness that would make Eagle feel about his falling

                        unhappy
        Stray Dog sat down and licked each sore paw
                    then trotted all night along
the edge of a highway and all morning along the edge

                    of a country road
            on one side empty barns on the other
                    side fields of upturned soil
on the edge of the highway as the burning headlights

                    illuminated
            him he couldn't see himself
                    on the edge of the country road
he saw a woman ride by on a bike and because she didn't stop

                    and put her hand out
            he didn't know if kindness
                    was a part of her it was
when she was a child she pulled a small owl off a barbed wire fence

                    without
            shedding a drop of blood
                    this isn't her story
Stray Dog grew tired and walked more than tired into an

                    empty barn
            it smelled of animals who had lived
                    and died at least side by side
he lay down in the corner and put his head between his paws

                                            Continued

                    listened
            to the dead who had lived
                    drag themselves across the straw floor
in the house of his own body he had an exact fear

                    of being harmed
            his eyes grew heavy he expected
                    never to wake up or else
to wake up in a human house with no door and one

                    window
            to look out of at the feeling
                    he had about the wind
that it was breaking the air into even more pieces

                    the next day
            a car grazed his hip
                    he trotted on until the pain felt
important and sat down on a bed of scattered rocks

                    wanting
            only to wait there until the sky felt
                    it could crouch down and touch him
with a hand and if this had happened he might have taken the hand

                    in his mouth
            and bit down with no idea
                    who cared to destroy him
time passed with no help from anyone he stood up no

                    miracle
            and started trotting again the farther
                    he trotted the weaker he felt
he saw that there were more trees now than before

      at sunrise
    at sunrise he had left the barn
       and now at noon the sun still
rising he was leaving the country road and entering a forest

       hungry
    with no end in sight just trees
       standing among each other
he saw a hole in the ground stuck his nose in it smelled flight

      from danger
    delirious he ran in search of Eagle
       thinking that if Eagle were dead
he would eat the body thinking that if Eagle were alive he would

      show
    wherever wings come from
       and wings themselves how to fly
his instinct moved him to slow down then his instinct

      fled from him
    then slowed down all the way
       and waited for him everything
and everyone alive around him as he lay down on his side

The Land of the Living

There's no guide book,
and the pages are stained with tears. You see,
already I'm not
making sense, when that's all
I rolled out of bed
to try and do.
The caution with which I opened
my eyes is still germinating,
slowly turning
every fiber of my being
into a shield
so circular that when I'm fully awake
I'll be on the edge of sleep, for lack
of a better expression.

Once, elbows
on a table in the half-lit
stacks of a library, chin up, I invented my own
cursory philosophy,
something about how the words
on the spines of a row of books
right before my eyes through the half-gloom
could purify any idea my interior self
could bemoan or sing or praise
or rip into, something about how the surface
could be a sea horse at the same time
the depth is a horse, something about how ...
Something about how ... The words were as if stuck like
barnacles to my teeth.

And I remembered as a boy lying beside the ocean
in the same driftwood tent
as my parents, two people
whose quietness kept giving
birth to my character, the roar of the waves
the lullaby I awoke to, my shoulders and back
numb, my legs driftwood .... I could feel who I was
radiating from the even tinier grains
of sand inside the grains of sand, the belly
of the whale inside the story, the moral
of which was ... I could feel all
knowledge giving me just enough nerve
to feel the sun radiating from my interior self and trying to spread
                                                            to my eyes,

for love of possible words.

And I remembered as a boy countless
trips to the zoo,
the orange tiger and the yellow lion
and the orange orangutan and the gray monkey
the colors of dawn,
in the sense that I believed
my mind was for articulating
how I hadn't evolved beyond them —
their wordless words were my words, if
you see what I mean.
The quietness of my mother, pointing.
The quietness of my father, pointing.
My quietness, if I only knew it, containing
the hope of generations,

Continued

precise, accurate enlightenment,
the cure discovered
and lost and rediscovered
over and over, a book
that maybe isn't there at all,
that is there but maybe never
opens, that is, not to my astonishment,
maybe always open, its inner light shining
up at me and getting through my stained eyes
and getting lost in my spine.
At any rate, there's certainly no death
while I'm sleeping or awake, no end
to the serenity of not knowing, and the calm
of knowing, while such calm lasts.

The Journals of Lewis and Clark

A wind squall as if
takes the tiller from Charbonneau
and drives the boat and everything
in it on its side.
Cruzatte, with all his strength,
rights it.

Sacagawea, her little son
on her back, reaches out for summaries
of whole days as they float away.

Lewis watches from shore,
helpless.
Clark explores the woods behind Lewis,
unaware.

Charbonneau regains the tiller. Cruzatte
begins bailing.

Sacagawea, waist deep, her little son
crying with both eyes, gathers summaries
of whole days before they float away.

What Do You Say?

All the lambs I met while walking in Britain in May
scampered away before I was within ten yards. All
except one, who within five yards stumbled, as if drunk,
right into my path, stopped in front of me, as I stopped,

and looked up at me the way a schoolchild looks up at the Queen.
What do you say to a lamb who's drunk on life, who's motor-skilled
his way into a position where you're more smell than aura,
more worthy of interest than of fear? Not much,

just a few clicks of the tongue, a little something extra
to indicate you're not only alive, but also alive.

An Inkling

Hovering outside the Time-Life building,
waiting until it was time to go up and meet
my childhood friend I hadn't seen in years
and take him out to lunch, I had an inkling

and it came apart at the seams. Even now,
months later, after I've had time to wonder,
I can't describe it. I can only as if
point to it, like, well, like a child

pointing at a wild creature in the zoo.
Technically, the child is also in the zoo,
but unrestrained, free. He's pointing
at bone, blood, muscle, wishing he could, well,

do something about it — I mean be closer to it,
hunt, feed with it, *exist* with it. All right,
I *can* describe it. I had an inkling
that two childhood friends embodied a life

so natural it's ridiculous — slinking
to Central Park, roaming Sheep's Meadow
in search of prey, slinking back toward
Time-Life, stopping to lurk outside

the Plaza Hotel, waiting for the meatiest
prey to emerge. So what does it
mean? That inklings are groundless?
Well, this one, at least. But what else?

I believe, as I was hovering there at
the very bottom, I conceived adulthood
and childhood as a few animal moments,
immediate, hungry. Then it was time to go up.

Child at Heart

The groundhog and the rabbit my child at heart
    friend says are friends
have crisscrossed her yard so many times this spring.

Will she be invited to their tea party?
    Behind which wall
of bushes lies their home with its miniature

stone fireplace, miniature earth-colored rug,
    miniature
black rocking chairs, miniature porcelain

cups and saucers, with its braided-together
    dandelion
roof, just tall enough for her?

"Lovely to see you," the groundhog will say, if
    she's invited,
extending his tiny hand, pulling her

gently inside, the loosely braided-together
    dandelions
letting the sunlight through, sunlight raining down

on her, the rabbit popping out of the kitchen,
    asking her what
sort of cookies she likes, they have all kinds.

To my imagination I see
    no limit.
Last Sunday I walked over to see her

and we sat outside and waited for the groundhog
   and the rabbit
to show. "Come on," she whispered, "come out,"

and soon the groundhog, if not the rabbit, appeared.
   "Look," she whisper-
screamed. He looked like a stuffed animal,

yet he moved, lumbering yet elegant, through
   the ankle-high grass,
his head whipping from side to side. He

spotted us and froze, no doubt in his
   bones that our wish
was to kill him, though every act we commit —

driving to work, driving back from the lake
   after a swim,
writing a check, reading a book, climbing into bed,

closing our eyes — keeps the sun that keeps us alive
   alive.

Lachrymose

In the first years of the second decade of
my life, I
had on my bedroom wall a poster of
a baby seal without
its skull crushed in, with its immaculate
fur, a more
spirited shade of white than the snow, intact,
with its big, liquid
eyes staring at the lens or at the face of
the photographer,
blue, blue sky a backdrop to die for.
The poster
taught me not to know what to do–revel
in breathless beauty? ...
mourn in advance? ... fall
through the solid ice
of irony and drown?

After a time, I removed
the poster from my consciousness, and it stayed
stuck to the wall without
my help, as always.
These days I read the newspaper as my vision
fades, watch the news
on T.V. as my vision fades — but these
are expected complaints that have lost their nerve.

May I go back years and years to the day
I took the poster down?
I don't remember an instant of that day.
What is possible?
Universal sunlight —
I don't remember that the room was filled with it.
I wish to go back, roll up
the poster, a flimsy telescope with
no power,
and put my hand on
the blank space, upon
which lies the genesis of evolution
and weaponry and
fur and profit and the immediate
divinity of compassion,
upon which lies an urge
to take universal and personal
sadness and make
them into music designed to take
eyes free of tears and
re-create them, an urge
at odds with the
overwhelming absence
of sadness — I know it's out there,
I know it's in me. But I can't see it.

The World

The World

I need to feel something for the place where I live.
Its walls. Its door. Its concrete path to the street.

Antarctica is pure no more — in so many words,
that's what the magazine lying closed on the floor says.

I sit in a chair by the window. In a photograph of me
smashed inside an album, the grass around my head, the skin

on my arms seems perfect. Outside, the wind covers
impossible distances, waves goodbye to the child

who stands under the clothesline in his backyard.
If he walked in the door I would hand him a little plastic truck

and a road to Antarctica the way it was before
the sewage, the chemicals, the oil.

He's standing so still. The road can't be traveled,
it's so narrow. I had the truck as a child,

no further. If I walked out the door, started down the concrete
or ice path, it doesn't matter, and crashed to my knees

pain is the something I would feel.

The Slaughter of Elephants

There is one truth
it is the used warm breath
flowing in storms from the long delicate nose
flowing from the small mouth without a word

It is also a cry
half trumpet half crude scream
half child who wants to be man
that we have grown to call music or impotence
and that is neither

Truth is not a part of language

It is not a part of the jeweled ivory tusks
flowered from the head ready to be picked
as if the skull is a mindless garden of roots

The poacher will tell you
he has taught his victim
the word for money for sacrifice
he will tell you the animal
went down on two knees
to articulate its weakness
he will tell you the bullets
obliterated the huge body
created an inner explosion
that resulted first in heart failure
and then in the merciful
burning of each scrap of breath
leaving the earth as it is
he will tell you
the sound the animal made
after the explosion
was an attempt at sound
an exceptional failure

(The Comanche
spoke to the buffalo
after they killed it
saying *please*
we too are dying
look through to our hunger
and our nakedness with your eyes
saying there is an actual world
in which death remains to feed on us)

There is one truth
anything is meant to be saved
flat earth
generations of the dead or dying
the elephant
smaller than a mountain
there is one truth
if they all disappear
ton by ton
the end of the world
which they would say has arrived
would be no occasion
for their huge spirits to rise
and profusely bless and bless

1987

The Hole in the Ozone Layer

If I could touch it as if
it was a gaping wound being
offered the cruel opportunity
to gape more, like a yawn
gone bad, splitting the edges
of the mouth until it's not
possible to cry out even
in useless despair,

I would feel tall for a moment,
for a moment my knees would lack
oxygen, gasp for breath, and
then fossilize, and then try
to startle themselves by
burying themselves above
headstones....Without these wild stabs
at anthropomorphizing even

my own body, the earth, with
its heart's core and its fake
hole in its stomach,
its equator running

right up its spine,
its ankles and eyes
dizzy with attitude and
impossible altitude, cares

even less for itself
than it does for me.

1995

Elegy for Dian Fossey

Her murder remains a mystery, her head sliced in two by one
of any number of people

who desired to prevent her
from saving the Mountain Gorillas of Central Africa,

their huge heads hacked off
and sold as souvenirs, their babies captured

and sold to zoos. One
rescued baby she nursed almost all the way back to health —

was somewhat surprised
to see the animal break down and sob.

○

I walk down an abandoned railroad track, stop, turn, walk up
to a barbed-wire fence,

look into a cow's eyes
and the face of the earth is not human.

A tree replaces my spine,
totters in the soil that crumbled through my fingers.

○

Continued

One gorilla walked up behind her and put his massive arm
gently around her shoulders ...

she grunted and munched
on a blade of grass ... she had spent half the night typing up notes,

all morning destroying traps ...
it was late afternoon ... she looked up at a ball of fire

in a sky strewn with unbreatheable planets.
The gently-around-her-

shoulders gorilla ended up murdered. His hands and head hacked off.
Years later she wrote:

I have tried
not to allow myself to think

of the total comprehension he must have suffered in knowing
what humans were doing to him.

Auras

I've been thinking of what a chimpanzee
trained to make words with his hands called
Alka Seltzer:
Listen Drink.

I've been thinking of Shakespeare's "The thousand natural shocks
That flesh is heir to," of how I feel
the shocks but they don't feel
natural.

I've been thinking of all this talk about saving Earth.
Rain forests, major rivers, wild animals are,
in my mind's eye, lined up
like bowling pins —

lately I've been going ahead and putting down
bad images like this.
But what I've been thinking of
most of all

is what I heard
nights ago
on Public Television: half of all dolphins
taken into captivity don't last more

than a few weeks, are
unable to adapt, or, as we say, unable
to move mountains,
commit suicide, some argue,

Continued

by simply shutting
off their systems.
I've been picturing
man made pools, like fetal oceans, like infant lakes.

I've been picturing those dolphins who *do* last,
who hold themselves
part way out of the water
and, with auras of immaculate

consolation, kiss their trainers on the lips.

A Photograph of Mount Rainer

> "Mont Blanc yet gleams on high: — the power is there,
> The still and solemn power of many sights,
> Many sounds, and much of life and death."
> Percy Bysshe Shelley

1.

"Forever," "natural" — two tired words I could
find brighter shadows of. Not now. Now
my eyes zero in on the summit and see
the sun rising only so far and drawing
a white cloud over its conflicts with itself.
I feel incomplete, but I find a modicum
of comfort in this: the mother tongue would die
a real death if it outgrew primal vision.

2.

Am I seeing or believing? The choice
melts at the base, leaving what remains
to arch its back as much as it can,
rise like snow and fall like new
snow onto the substance already
blanketing. My ankles are buried,
and yet how can I be there, above
the base, slowly walking, slowly scaling
or climbing, the fluid wind the same
icy word toppling my shoulders and
leaving my heart-region standing?
Sunlight so close to the sun doesn't
gravitate toward uncertainty, lead
to questions that, if asked, are millions

Continued

of miles away. The snow, so cold, so
itself, knows the core of my ankles,
how to see toward it, how to stay with it
until frostbite sets in, leading to
the absence of pain after and even

3.

before amputation. Scaling somehow
horizontally — that's what believing is like.
I can't see where I am. Below the base,
a knife, and a tree, and a human heart
realized to make it look carved lead farther
down to the initial, peaceful trappings
of society radiating out toward cities
constructed in the eye's mother tongue
in the hope of reconciling incomprehensible
power with occupiable buildings, of
replacing soil and rock never touched
directly by rain with buried conduits,
and in the strange hope of replacing snow
too cold to breathe with buried or visible
power lines. I see the mountain and don't understand
why it allows everyone into its arms,
only to stop them at its chest.

4.

Impregnable, the heart-region inside
a body with no heart. Contemplating
this body so grand it's truly a mountain
hurts so much. Not too long ago, it lived
removed and therefore acted as a source
of uncommon serenity. Because society grows

so close now to where heaven will never
lean down to welcome them into its fold,
nature feels mortal, like a blank without
an ever-fresh grace, a blank that only
the laying on of human hands can heal,
and only if the heart of contemplation —
political action — is taken. I've lost
my thread. The mountain involves itself not
in rhetoric as I gaze at it, but in
poetry that sends my knees down and then
topples them, that lets me live by half-
creating me, my other half standing
and writing lines that congratulate themselves
for leaving nature unchanged. And so I'm back
to where I'm always dying toward: rhetoric.

5.

It can't be helped. The world condition
has become the human condition. We can't
just gaze, and language, like a photograph
of a human atrocity resistant to fire, can't
wash away its own sins. "Darkness,"
"silence" — without us, the words would remain,
it seems, and yet they're afraid, it seems,
to let us go. Who are we, if of "darkness"
there is no brighter shadow?

Why Did the Turtle Cross the Road?

So it could pause halfway, as if breathless,
and elicit a little pity from passing
motorists. So passing motorists could
feel themselves skimming along the surface
of life with no shell holding them down, as if flying
over burning coals and electric fences.
So passing motorists could feel how rife
their lives are with the greatest of ease,
how laughably remote nature can be
through their eyes, how lightly terrible.
The rest of the distance took forever,
one near miss after another. So it could
pause at the far edge of the road, as if free
of all cruelties and blessings and jokes.

True Love

On the road out of here there's a little museum
packed with dinosaur bones and no one

but the owner knows why. His white hair falls
into his bloodshot eyes. Any money you give him

he gives to the pail below the busted register.
According to local legend, not only was he an orphan

but his only girlfriend kept him waiting forever
outside a movie theater, two tickets in his hand,

a breeze motioning to his heart to come out
from under his body and break against the sidewalk.

The museum used to be a Dairy Queen. Inside,
there's nothing to eat or drink, there's history

seen through bloodshot eyes tired of closing
and opening like machines. The one time I visited,

one glass case, the bones inside the size
of scepters or crowbars, led me to imagine an elk

uneasy entering the Ark beside a caribou.
I wish I was writing this in the tavern up the road

from the museum, reaching across a table
to slap him on the back the way friends do, spilling

Continued

my beer, swearing and laughing. Friends we're not
and so I don't know if the stories about him are true.

He never even looked at me, let alone confided:
I gazed into the past before I realized it's impossible

saw dinosaurs lying across the ground like hills
gasping like fish their eyes envisioning me their mouths

giving birth to me their eyes breathing me back in
not only was I an orphan but my only girlfriend

offered me in place of true love a single bone.

Extinct

1740. The Bering Sea. A species
that had existed for countless years
was given a name: Steller's Sea Cow.
These creatures protected each other and they were strong —
to kill one for food Steller's men
had to kill twenty. Over the next twenty-
seven years they would all be killed.
They are all frozen, now, in the human mind. No cure in sight.

○

How to describe a Steller's Sea Cow?
Not like a cow at all;
thirty feet long; 14,000 pounds; face like a walrus'
without tusks; arms like a human's arms broken
at the elbow; toothless; tail like a fish's; unrelated
to the whale; brother to the elephant; one day
heaved itself off the land and began to swim;
a hook the size of an anchor lodged in its back;
dead.

○

Who cares?
If I walk out my door and onto the highway
and stop the cars
no one will get home.
We have come to a conclusion:
if we recognize the extinct
they will not stop crying.
Humans cry, to make room for hunger.
These creatures go down deeper for air,
bread and water behind their eyes.

Nature Poem

Here's why I need to stand here
in this meadow
as the smell of grass
rises to my hips, as
a humble servant —
a footprint's worth of
blades — lies smashed under
each of my shoes:
My head up high, my arms
dropped down as far
as they'll go, I'm
the carving removed
from the wood, the
blank without the
canvas. And still
the feel of grass so
deep under
that it's finished growing
rises.

In Pursuit of a Theme

Animal Behavior

We sit in our apartments and consider our lives.
Nature has no concern for us.

We have concern for nature.
Grazed field upon grazed field,

declining towns and cities like beds
of imitation flowers lie between us.

Joy has no concern for me. I have concern for joy.
Inside your own walls, behind your own window,

unhappy, your life devoured,
I think you understand.

O

I read yesterday in a book on animal behavior

about a young dolphin who, when attacked
by three sharks, began to whistle, shrilly, higher and higher,

shrilly and coldly. Twenty dolphins or more
swam into the sharks. The sharks, their skeletons

shattered, sank to the bottom of the Caribbean Sea.
The young dolphin, wounded, without the strength

to rise to the surface and replace the air
in his body, floated down. Two dolphins

Continued

positioned themselves on either side of him,
placed their flippers under him, raised him up,

eased him down, raised him up, day and night, for two weeks,
until the wounds were healed.

        O

I say all wounds heal. Your wound
will not heal. Therefore, you wound does not exist.

Lean on your walls. Make no mistake: I have a wound:
go to your window to see if it is there:

it is gone.

Shelter

Auden called the houses of the poor
sorry vegetation.

I don't know what to call them.
The houses of the poor

are like bodies of water.
Should the rain stop, I will go for a walk,

see, in the back of one of houses
of the poor,

a goat tied to a bare tree, stretching the rope
as far as it goes,

kneeling like a camel
in the sopping grass, the dense clouds

shelter from the moon, the lifeless planets,
the stars, the sun.

Tess of the D'Urbervilles

I picture her hacking turnips out of the ground for a living.
She's so forsaken, so ordinary,

so confused, she could be anyone.
She's worked her hands to death. No, she's stopped to breathe

on them, they're so cold.
Hunched over the rain-soaked, flowerless ground,

she's as beautiful
as the streaks of dirt across her wrists, the absence of blood.

She's making little money.
Nature doesn't owe anyone anything.

I picture her lost in the woods, making a bed out of leaves,
waking up, half-dead

pheasants lying all around her. She finishes them off
out of compassion,

walks on, at last finds work hacking turnips out of the ground.
She can't see her future:

her early death, her five soft nights
against her husband's body.

Hunched over the rain-soaked, flowerless ground,
she feels her heart

has slowed to a crawl, and I believe her because I'm tired,
working day in, day out

inside a building for little money.
No comparison.

The Ocean

    after Rachel Carson

I arrived after dark, got a motel room, and in the morning
went downstairs like an anchor, sat in the restaurant.
Language, for me, was sand, words grains. I couldn't even begin
to understand what the waitress was asking me. I exaggerate.
The beach was a short drive away, the water extending out
as far as the eye can see, touching the sky — an illusion,

like my sense that because I was alone
I wasn't related, wasn't like all people
who began their lives in a miniature ocean within
their mother's womb, metaphorically repeating the steps
by which gill-breathing inhabitants of a water world evolved into
creatures able to live on land.

Later, there I was, at the edge. Waves fell flat
and touched the tips of my shoes. I pictured a barefoot
child shrieking and dancing backwards. I crouched down
and sacrificed a hand. The water was cold all right.
To say I was alone as I stood beside the ocean
I couldn't live in — is that right? To say I was alone as I stood
beside the ocean, the waves like exhausted swimmers cresting
                                                toward me
and disintegrating before I could save them — that's not right. To say
I was alone as I drove back to the motel, went upstairs
like an anchor, tried to sleep — but first I strolled
beside forbidden tears until darkness fell
and the stars in the sky became themselves.

In Pursuit of a Theme

At the ocean I take driftwood and sand
and build a house with a glass roof and stand
outside of it and gaze up at the stars.

In the nearby town I combine the empty pots
in the window of a closed shop with the dirt
from under my fingernails, and produce as many wildflowers
as there are reasons to live.

What am I getting at?
Like a symbol we lay, my first
love and I, on a rug
in front of a fireplace. We stood
for the pain we had not
yet caused each other. Outside, it
was snowing. How did it
happen? One flake led to another
and our lips touched.

Back home from the ocean, I turn on the TV,
flip through the channels, and there it is: a crab
threatening the camera with its huge claw,
its flat body the color of an orange just ripe enough to sell.

So what? You see, I desire no
separation between
interior and exterior.
With these lies I hope to
persuade you my desire knows no bounds.

I live in a house that's crumbling to the ground.
I gaze up at the bedroom ceiling and
accept the rain. It is written in the stars.

My new love and I imagine a stretch of land
no one but us has ever set eyes on.
We wish to build a house there with
no gate, nothing to lock or even close,
a house as exposed as a blade of grass.
We won't be surprised if we plant trees inside of it.
In the immense backyard will be
the garden, a place in the world where
it's much less difficult for us to grow,
to ripen, to give ourselves over to hunger.

One spring night you will
walk right through the door and see us
lying apart on a bare floor.
Look closer and you will see her tears
on my lips. There

will always be something between us. And
it will never be a wall. And winter
on that stretch of land my come twice a year
but we will never clean the fireplace.

The Living

You think sunrise is more beautiful
I think sunset

The street outside our house
blue-black in the sun
is like a whale risen just
enough to breathe

After you fall asleep
I get desperate for like
to become is
go outside and spread my hands
over your half of the ocean

I could swear I wake with your hands
over my eyes
you've been up
for hours sinking
sinking breathing
without me

The greatest elegy couldn't even begin

to express how the living
miss each other

compensate for each other
encompass a whole day

The One Church

I enter
through a door the height of two of me.

Long ago,
the altar was delivered up
to the cave above the horizon.

There is an empty tract of land
that has, itself, nowhere to go,
and the path to it is the nave.

Edges of pews bordering.

Vaulted ceiling supporting
by watching over edges.

Hearing behind me equal numbers of ribs swimming
in breath enough for three of me,
I stop halfway.

Straight ahead, through stained glass strayed
from its true place by its own
volition, and not on the four wings
of a windstorm that was once countless
particles of air congregated around
the horizon above the cave, I see the altar
floating back down, reflecting back
to my eyes, spreading to my sides
and over edges.

Below the structure,
there is a tract of land.

For the life of it, pews fill.

God and Nature

As I look across the river to the apartment complex,
all of its windows the same but separate, even
under cloudcover like brilliant versions of God,
and the river the one and only version, too simple
to understand, and the slight breeze like a compass
that blows in a direction it doesn't indicate, I feel
I live everywhere, behind this window, or that

window — no need to point to what I know by
transparent shade pulled down over myriad heart.
Standing on my feet, at a good distance from my hands,
perhaps I live, opening all barriers after
I hear the sound of my knuckles on the other side,
and before in my mind that knows all the known facts
and gives birth, like each new child, to more.

Here I am, though, turning away and beginning
again to walk the path along the river. Of myself
I'm no version. Just beneath my surface
I float. As I was looking, looking was an opiate,
and my blood's path was like the mercury
inside a thermometer that measures both body
and shelter, everyone welcome, even

the faceless one, whose face is just a river.

First Visit to Walden Pond

> "The comfort we need is inhuman."
>   Bill McKibben, *The End of Nature*

I can't even begin

to describe the water. I know the parking lot,
the children, the either plain or psychedelic

towels and two-piece bathing suits and swimming trunks
and the lifeguard tower like the back of my hand.

I go walking and come to a small rectangle
of earth, a chain around it, where Thoreau's house stood.

Since his death, thousands of leaves and petals have landed
on his face. How sick I am of imagination.

I want, as Thoreau suggested, to reduce
it to understanding. The thousands of petals

and leaves that have fallen through his death mask
must be recovered. Obviously, I'm not

sick enough of imagination to stop using it.
It's almost funny how every day thousands more

people than there are parking spaces at Walden
take down his book and wish so badly that they could

have built beside his house a house as tiny
as a seed. I turn around and walk to the edge of

the water. I ask the morning star — his name
for the sun — to make me invisible to one who,

any moment now, will walk up beside me, crouch
down, fill his hands, wash out his eyes, one who,

in so many words, believed we all should have our own
body of water. It's no good. On my way back

to the parking lot, I keep running into him.
He winces. He reaches out and puts his hands

over my face. I peek through his fingers and hear
children in the distance splashing and screaming.

Love the children less than nature? We've all done time
in prison asking questions. We need to imagine

that Thoreau, rather than protecting a daughter
or a son, caught the acid before it hit the water.

And I suppose we need to imagine
that the water loved him back.

Second Visit to Walden Pond

Less shattered

by the irony of the ultimate symbol
    of solitude turned into
a public beach, I join the crowd and swim,
    only once turning on my back
and facing the empty sky.

I don't swim well at all, so I stick to water
    I can stand up in, so I'm
surrounded by children in pairs playing
    shark, one digging his nails into
the other's leg, the other bursting to the surface and shrieking.

After I change in the awful, just awful
    bathroom, dutifully, almost
reluctantly, I walk along the edge
    of the water, people
sunbathing or reading in each small cove,

some twisting their necks to eye me peacefully,
    some obviously trying
to shut me out.
    Arriving at the small
rectangle of earth, a chain around it,

where Thoreau's house stood, I imagine
    children protecting the beach,
showing their teeth, imagine Styrofoam cups
    and plastic knives picked up, removed,
replaced, picked up.

Continued

I walk around the rectangle, clockwise, once,
    and then begin retracing my steps.
Just for fun, I pretend I'm him — I've just
    woken up and I'm splashing
water on my face. And then I hear

the couple behind me agonizing over
    the difficult dynamic
exclusive to their hopelessly distinct
    natures, or personalities.
I walk so slowly that they pass by me.

There's some slogan on the back of his T-shirt,
    nothing, of course, on the back
of her sun dress.
    Her bare arms are breathtaking.
His bare arm desperately clings to her waist.

Green

Cycle

Those winter days, walking
outside, when I seek out
a sunlit sidewalk, and then
it might as well be
a seasonless world,

where most everyone —
everyone — wants
violence to drown in peace,
wants violence to
go gently, made as it

might as well be
out of the concept
that shuns it — nothing
can breathe itself.

Those summer days, walking
outside, when I put my hand out
to stop a few drops
from hitting the sidewalk, and then
the partial — the whole —

aim of gravity isn't
drenched in futility,
though futility might
as well be what I feel.
Those seasonless nights,

waking to a world versed
in terror and despondency,
when dead leaves and
withered blossoms

already warm as our blood
come in from the cold.

Green

I think I'm a found soul, walking
past a mound of dead leaves, embedded
in it a liquor bottle inside

a paper bag the color of dead leaves, I think
I'm a found soul, I don't believe.
Where am I? Where I am could be

the world as it is, where I am is
the world as it could be, where
the color green can't wait

for its rebirth. And where I'm going
is the heaven beyond heaven, the heaven beyond
set objects littered with space and time.

Walking past a mound of dead leaves, lying
on top of it the front page of a newspaper
saturated in yesterday's rain, I don't believe, I don't believe

I can go so far
as to turn news the texture of tears through
my eyes back

into absolute suffering.

Blight

Few cars in the parking lot
at Robert E. Lee's birthplace
on a Friday afternoon,

and only two horses,
the wood fence surrounding them
strung with barbed wire,

the rain touching them equally,
falling diagonally, like wind.
Early April, and the wildflowers

are almost as tall as the grass.
Hundreds of robins fly over the garden
in the direction of the burial vault.

A few yards north of the brick house
lie the remains of a springhouse
and a shallow stream

where the young boy sat
and dreamed a mile through
chestnut trees to the Potomac,

a long dream of unparted water.
Thirty-five years after Appomattox
the trees perished

in the chestnut blight.
Some stand in the imagination,
more dead than ever.

Some go on surrendering their leaves
in a place the rain will never touch
as long as there is war.

24 Hours

My own happiness seems unimportant.
I say *seems*.
I wouldn't lie to you.
I'm not the one
without food or shelter.
I wouldn't run a knife across your back
until you asked for my forgiveness.
My own happiness is a room
with no windows
and an open door.
Every morning I close my eyes
and face east.
To my amazement, which the years
have dulled,
the sun rises.
It takes all day
and all night.
But sometimes I get it in my head
that 24 hours
is one moment of despair,
in which my front tires
kiss the squirrel
and I, with everywhere to go,
veer off the mountain road
and begin the descent back.

Sioux Hunters: Photograph by Edward S. Curtis

There are three horses, one black, one white, one
an impossible blending of the two,
as if struck by its own sun — and three riders,
one obscured by the black horse's neck, one man
wearing a heavy shawl, and one man
who appears to be his own shadow.
They are waiting, the impossible horse
turned away, the black horse and the white horse
facing the camera, their riders
looking at something the photograph
doesn't contain, their heads
titled back, as if they're trying to stay awake.

If the photograph wasn't so beautiful I would say it's out of focus.
The stones appear to be trembling.
unafraid, and the mountain range is a monstrous wave subsiding
from the land where nothing grows
save short, hard grass.

I have no idea what the hunters are hunting for.

And this sense of peace — I can't explain it: it's as if
the horses breathed me in, as if I buried my face
in the shawl, as if the mountains have risen like a wave
and carried this image into the future, as if the future
is barren, uninhabitable, merciful, primitive.

My Mind's Eye

I'm always granting my mind's eye
leave to go. And always I'm insisting
it stay. For instance, when I walk my dog
on the empty land where the new
high school will go, I see the rich,
uncut grass the way I'll see it inside
me when it's gone, and also
see it now, receive it now,
plainly, like a crust of bread,
as if otherwise I would go
hungry forever.
                    My mind's eye
has never known hunger, continually
restores itself. With my help? Can I
insist it stay? Can I grant it leave to go?
Or do I simply exist within its sway?
What have I ever done
to cultivate in me what seems to keep me
alive?
      It's not
that I will compensate for the grass
when it's gone. It's that
when it's gone I'll see inside me a hand fishing
through ashes, a hand that's been burning
for as long as I can remember.

A Dog's Life

I'm in love with the life of a dog.
I want to sleep, wake up, sleep
all day, every day. I want to be
the withheld, helpless breath.
If it means running free over the sidewalk
I want a triangle of glass in my paw.
I want to ignore my wound, my birth,
let my blood flow from one vein
to another. I want to gallop toward
a stranger, and I want the stranger
to put his hand, smelling of fear,
on my head and laugh. I want
to piss on a gravestone, define
happiness as hard rain I, without hope,
can bear. I want the wind, the drifting
clouds, even the motionless ground,
to make promises and say nothing
about whether they will keep them.
Crying out like a small child when
left alone in the human world, an empty
room, I don't want heaven. I want to be
interested in all food, chew the rotten
meat, suck up its juice because it's
better than hunger, better than a clear
stream. Whoever comes to me, I want
to always stay with them, look through
them with soulless eyes, put my head
gently on their knee so as not to hurt them.
I want to love, I who can't love.

With Loneliness

Sick — there is no other word —
with loneliness,
I sit inside a pasture, watching cows

inch toward me. I will be eaten.
They inch closer and closer.
They gather around me.

They leave me alone.
I try the grass — bittersweet.
I caw like a crow. One cow,

his ribs showing, turns to me, moos,
but nothing he can say
can help me

except: You are one of us.

Whale Watching

We wait by the lighthouse that stands on a cliff above the beach.

One woman
stands so still, her windbreaker filled like a sail —

I half-believe
she'll be blown out to sea, she'll disappear beneath the surface.

One man in shorts holds his binoculars up to his eyes
with one hand,

stands so still he looks paralyzed, hungry
for the world to take place.

I look at the beach, can't help
but notice the scattered driftwood, see, below

the tideline, a grain of water
enclosed within a grain of sand but I'm not looking hard enough.

I don't know
which species cruises along this coast

or how far down
their backs the breathing hole is or why some claim they can't love.

Though I would drown, I'm sorry
I can't walk into the ocean that hoards and hoards and promises
to give ....

Continued

It's almost time to go home ....

It's time to go home ....

Home is a dark wave
that could be the back of a whale, that can't be,

that must be
the reason I've waited so long for nothing.

Sentimentality

All last spring, all around
the wooded area
where I live, clear-cutting:
the controlled creation
of absence in the face
of unsentimental
necessity.

I wonder now if all
last winter and fall and
summer I should have gone so far
as to feel the stumps to be
souls with no nature,
no mother ....

It's spring again, and I'm
trying to allow
myself to lose my battle
with sentimentality,
trying to clear

my wood house of its wood
to see what letting in an
unbridled human element
might accomplish ....

All around the area
where I live, and inside me:
stumps that once were
stumps and nothing more,
and human emotion that
never will tower above
what's reasonable and appropriate.

Romantic

Tree Farm

It's just across the road. No cars.
Walk across in the silence of soles

on dirt, and on the other side make
the grass whisper as you crush it

and let it go, crush it and let it go....
Then make your unannounced entrance.

Such an unoriginal, rich fragrance.
Such neat rows. Such slenderness.

Just breathing might cause falling
and disarray. Anyway, breathe as if

nothing will happen, save that your chest
will grow slender as you inhale,

save that waiting for you to exhale
will be the next breath in line, there

since the advent of the inception.

Glen Nevis

How sane we are to be willing
to walk for miles to get to the exact, beyond
beautiful landscape in our mind.

Seven miles and here I am, basking
in the sound of a mild river
running through a tiny canyon

shaded by wind-bent trees shaded
by craggy hills — all this
was like a flower pressed between

the pages of a book on Scotland until I opened
the book and dreamed of living
inside a photograph and closed

and waited years and flew thousands
of miles and rode a train hundreds and walked a hard seven.
A sheep canters into view,

then is gone, replaced by two
mountain bikers — they were
most certainly not

part of the flower, but I
find myself waving to them.
They wave back, and then are gone.

Over the mild sound
of the river, I can just hear
the cars going farther and farther

into the glen, breezing past beyond
beautiful landscape after beyond
beautiful landscape on their way

to the one that feels right.

Lines

    Composed a few miles above Rydal Mount

How many times I've tried to describe
to myself how Wordsworth saw Nature
as a concept, as a moral force through which
our worthiest actions are reflected.
Now that I'm here, a few miles above his house,
it seems less a matter of description
than of presentation. All around me
are green hills and yellow-green trees taking
my breath away, then bringing it home — I can't
bring myself to go on trying to describe
this pure, pure feeling I have right now,
or what worthy actions I'm more than hoping
to commit. Perhaps Wordsworth wished a poem
could simply be a map to where the poem
takes place, to where the words actually live right
before the eyes and thrill the heart into cleansing
the soul — here it doesn't matter how that works;
it just is. Tomorrow I'll be gone. And
a week from now I'll be back in my own country,
taking his poems off the shelf and seeing
each one as a shrine that's lost its way
and trying to see the whole book as a concept
and trying to see that I opened
it with the moral force of my hands.

Above Grasmere

    For my mother

After many days of traveling with you in Scotland
and England by car and train, and still more to go,
I've left you behind to rest, and hiked all this way, past
a wooden gate so easily opened, past a sheep perched
on a grassy outcrop of rock, past a roofless, so clearly
abandoned stone house that to the eye is indefinable
beauty itself, in the mid-May mist, in my thin-soled shoes
I've hiked all this way, past evermore bird's eye views,
on a broad path of green and rust-colored grass defined
by two slightly undulating stone walls more gorgeous
than perfect, the mist growing stronger as the path
unfolded, past a lone tree on a hillside, a lone tree
so clearly itself against a blank wall of white concealing
all the life down below, in my thin but adequate sweater
I've hiked all this way, through rain so light I didn't believe it
                                                                             was falling,
past breaks in the mist revealing what the lone tree so often
sees with the soul of its eyes ... the small, graceful town and
surrounding farms, the lake with its small, tree-filled island,
occasional breaks growing longer, past the many views
of the fabled, tangible, rust-colored and green mountain, slowly,
with all my racing heart I've hiked all this way to say
I imagine you down there in the town, gracefully swerving,
after musing long, away from Wordsworth's grave, alive to the
                                                                                 highest extent.

Romantic

Amid the din of towns and cities
I abide by a forest whose spirit

I half-create. Plenty of sunlight
filters in. Looking at the thick bark is like

looking down from the sky at a cluster
of islands separated by channels.

Breathing in is like drinking salt
water turned into fresh. The wind

picks up, and the crowns of the trees
lean to one side. The channels

are half-drunk, always. The wind
pauses in mid-flight. I wake, and

the din is as loud as ever. I'm fine
as long as this forest, this mortal

release, is just a dream's length away.

Nature Lover

I drive to the National Park,
walk through the trees, dropping my car key
somewhere on the shadowy ground,
and arrive at a clearing,
like a pool with excellent

swimmers standing around its edge,
sunlit dirt and moss the poor can walk on.
My shirt has short sleeves.
My jeans have no knees.
My wrists slip off like bracelets

and make no sound as they hit the dirt.
Feeling alive isn't
a feeling, exactly, it's more
a gut thought that wouldn't let go
even if the fire slid off

my eyes and ran down
my stomach and down
my shins and died.
I turn back and begin the search.
Even as the key

shines up at me and fits
sharply inside my fist,
even as
the thoughtless
engine starts,

I don't feel empty.

My Pasture

Who owns it I don't know.
I walk the old logging road through the woods as far
as the metal gate and look out onto empty space,
in the middle one tree that's really two trees branching
off from each other at the base, many other trees
forming a ragged circle around the mud-flecked grass.
Sometimes there are cows, and it's still empty as far
as my eyes are concerned. Nothing against cows.
If I climbed over the gate and stepped onto that grass,
I, too, would be lost and chewing as I stared blankly
in my direction or completely and utterly ignored me.
After a time, I begin to feel that the very first time
I reached the gate and, after a time, retraced my steps,
not exactly, I did everything Earth asked of me.
What Heaven consists of I know, just as I know
knowledge can't be owned.

The Woman at the Washington Zoo

>   after Randall Jarrell

At the Washington Zoo, months after I fell in love
with simply you, I fell in love with the way
you watch primates. This is what happens. Love grows
specific. First there's no reason. Then there are so many
it hurts. But concentrating on one at a time helps.

So there we were, at the zoo, on a balmy Saturday,
on a whim, and we came to the primate area,
a series of rooms, each with one wall of glass.
The way you watched the gorilla I remember best.
He was sitting near the glass, with his back half-turned,

and you walked right up to him and knelt down
to his adopted level, not like a child bent on
getting the animal's attention, but like a human
animal whose own attention was blessed, and who
possessed no other need than to bask in a shadow.

I stood an insignificant distance away from you,
feeling so awake to my desire to not disturb.
As fifteen minutes of our lifetimes, maybe less,
passed, I kept expecting at least a small portion
of your body to move. No. Your elbows as still as glass,

your shoulder blades under your blouse not betraying
the fact that you were breathing. And the gorilla?
He raised his hand once to scratch under his eye, his eye
not flinching — right there harmony would have
crystallized, except that you and I were free to flow

back out into the world, leaving the wild behind.

Yes

I appreciate the war against emptiness
in February. I'm not even thinking of
plant life, just the gray light on an average day
in February that permeates a city street,
like the controlled atmosphere inside a mall
gone bad. I assume control, and my control
amounts to nothing, like purchase power
reduced to zero, to the point that even my eyes
feel gray. I don't surrender. Shop windows seen
through dim natural light in February are
immaterial blessings. Turning the streetlights
on, though the moon hasn't materialized,
isn't the answer. Yes is the answer,
yes to the gray light, the sun's diluted

offspring, the rootless child with no delusions that never fears.

Chant

These early spring days, when the absurdity of existence
is cast in logical sunlight, when "absurdity" is a word
made out of the teeth of an infant, and "logical" is
like the way I can say I could gawk at the woman
outside the restaurant planting daffodils in the wooden
boxes around the useless in winter seating area all day.
Planting won't take all day. It may be evening before
"planting" finds a soft spot on my tongue and beds down —

out of the teeth of an adult arise certain
self-doubts. I'm sorry. Now that I'm an adult, maybe
it's a mistake getting abstractions to come out and play.
Focus on the woman, her existence the yellow in the flowers
the sun has spoken for, her green work shirt and blue jeans
all she owns in the maze of air that moves with her as
she moves from one box to the next, her spade the property
of its affinity with the soil. Is that any better? These

early spring days, when one apology simply leads to
another, and the first one can't find its way back home.
The woman is more than halfway through, and I think I have
a few more beats of the world's great heart before my
gawking starts to look strange to the world outside my world.
These early spring days, when existence in any form is free
up to a point, and after that protocol arises
like new science, of which I'll soon know more than nothing.

About the Author

Douglas Nordfors was born in Seattle in 1964. He has a BA from Columbia University and an MFA from The University of Virginia. He has published poems in many journals, including *The Iowa Review*, *Poetry Northwest*, *Poet Lore*, *Seattle Review* and *Quarterly West*, and taught writing and literature at Milton Academy, The University of Virginia, and James Madison University.

www.ingramcontent.com/pod-product-compliance
Lightning Source LLC
Chambersburg PA
CBHW071838290426
44109CB00017B/1852